W0007456

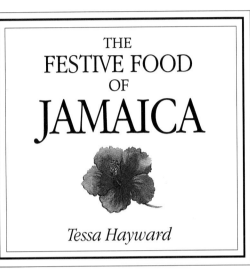

THE
FESTIVE FOOD
OF
JAMAICA

Tessa Hayward

ILLUSTRATED BY SALLY MALTBY

This book was personally commissioned by Boerries H. Terfloth, director of B. Terfloth & Co., partner with Grace, Kennedy & Co. Ltd. in Terfloth & Kennedy Ltd.

Gratefully acknowledged is Dr Olive Lewin, Arts & Culture Director, Grace, Kennedy & Co. Ltd., whose tremendous contribution made this publication possible.

Distributed in Jamaica by: Caribbean Greetings Ltd., subsidiary of Grace, Kennedy & Co. Ltd., Kingston.

CONGRATULATIONS TO GRACE, KENNEDY & CO. LTD. ON ITS 75TH ANNIVERSARY.

KYLE CATHIE LIMITED

The author and publisher wish to thank Dr. Olive Lewin, Arts and Culture Consultant of Grace, Kennedy & Co. Ltd., Kingston, Jamaica, for her extensive help with the preparation of this book. Dr. Lewin won a scholarship to the Royal Academy of Music, London, and has since worked widely in the field of arts, founding the Jamaican Orchestra for youth, as well as researching Jamaica's Folk Heritage. She served as a director of Art & Culture in the office of the Prime Minister 1981-1988. She has a weekly column in <u>Sunday Gleaner</u>.

First published 1996 by
Kyle Cathie Limited
20 Vauxhall Bridge Road, London SW1V 2SA

ISBN 185626240 5

A CIP catalogue record for this book is available from the British Library

Book design by Geoff Hayes
Jacket photography by Gregory Lopez

Colour origination by Positive Colour Ltd.
Printed through World Print Ltd., Hong Kong

Strawberry Hill Hotel Resort,
Blue Mountains

Pumpkin

Contents

New Year's Day

1ST JANUARY

Jamaica is the ravishingly beautiful sunshine island that has bewitched so many. The people, with their large smiles and love of life, have imbued the island with a wonderfully happy atmosphere.

There is always time for a festival or party, and at New Year the Islanders families get together and celebrate with music, dancing, singing and kissing on the stroke of twelve.

Roasted Breadfruit

The breadfruit, which originated in Polynesia, was brought to Jamaica by Captain Bligh of *Mutiny on the Bounty* fame. He arrived from Tahiti on *H.M.S. Providence* on 5th February 1793, with 347 breadfruit trees. These trees, which were imported with the intention of supplying food for the slaves, have the texture of potatoes. To obtain a delicious smoky flavour roast the breadfruit over glowing charcoal; otherwise put it under a hot grill.

8

1 Place each breadfruit on the barbecue or under the grill. As the fruit begins to blacken turn regularly until it is charred all over.
2 Cook for about an hour, or until steam starts to escape from the stem end.
3 Remove from the heat, cut a circle at the stem end and scoop out and discard the seeds.
4 Cut off the charred outer skin, slice the fruit and eat while hot.

Rum Punch

The famous drink of the island. With this ditty, it is an easy recipe to remember: one of sour, two of sweet, three of strong and four of weak. The men, when drinking together, will often spice it up by adding a few drops of hot pepper sauce.

1 part fresh lime juice
2 parts strawberry syrup
   or sugar syrup flavoured
   with a little grenadine
3 parts rum
4 parts water
sugar, to taste

1 Mix all the ingredients in a jug or container. Taste and add some sugar if desired.
2 Serve in glasses with ice and garnished with fresh fruit, if liked.

Saltfish and Ackee

New Year's Day starts with a breakfast of saltfish and ackee. This is almost the national dish of Jamaica, and has been eaten since the ingredients arrived on the island in the 18th century. Salt cod was imported from New England and each slave was presented with a yearly allowance of the fish.

The ackee tree came to Jamaica from tropical West Africa in 1778; five years later, a tree was taken by Captain Bligh to England where it was given its botanical name *Blighis Sapida* in his honour.

The ackee grew and flourished in Jamaica, and almost everyone grows one. The tree produces a flamboyant pendulous red fruit which bursts on ripening to reveal three large shiny black seeds, each of which is attached to an edible yellow aril. Unripe or over-ripe ackees are poisonous and the fresh fruit must be carefully prepared; as a result, it is now frequently sold in cans.

Ackees can also be served with smoked salmon or as an accompaniment to scrambled eggs, to make a change from the traditional saltfish and ackee.

225g/8oz saltfish
24 ackees or 1 x 500g/18oz can ackee
120g/4oz salt pork, diced
100ml/3½fl oz/⅓ cup coconut oil or
    vegetable oil
3 spring onions, chopped
3 medium onions, chopped
3 cloves garlic, chopped
½ scotch bonnet pepper, cored,
    deseeded and finely chopped
3 tomatoes, peeled and diced
½ teaspoon ground black pepper
2 or 3 sprigs thyme

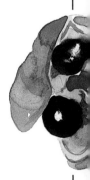

1 Soak the saltfish in cold water for several hours.
2 Remove the seeds and membranes from the
ackees and wash thoroughly. Place them in a pan of
cold salted water and bring to the boil. Simmer for
20 minutes or until tender, then drain. If using
canned ackees, drain and reserve.
3 Drain and rinse the saltfish, place it in a pan and
cover with water. Bring to the boil and simmer for
25 minutes or until cooked. Drain, remove and
discard all skin and bones, then flake the fish.
4 Fry the diced pork in a frying pan until crisp, then
remove and drain on kitchen paper.
5 Add the oil to the fat in the pan and sauté the
spring onions, onions, garlic and pepper until
softened. Add tomatoes, black pepper and thyme
and cook for another 3 minutes. Add the saltfish,
ackees and pork and cook, stirring gently, until hot.

Air Jamaica is the island's most popular airline and
passengers can be transported there with the
warmth of a true Jamaican welcome, in the luxury
the airline prides itself on offering. Louis Bailey is Air
Jamaica's chef and this is his:

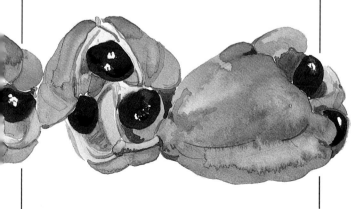

Jamaican Ackee Soup

50g/2oz butter
120g/4oz/½ cup Irish potato
50g/2oz onion
50g/2oz spring onions
1 x 250g/9oz can ackee (or 12 fresh ackee)
1.25l/2 pints/5 cups chicken stock

1 Melt the butter in a heavy bottomed pan and add
the finely chopped potato, onion and spring onion.
Cook gently for 2 minutes.
2 Add the ackee and chicken stock, and simmer for
20 minutes, blend all the ingredients to a purée,
taste for seasoning and serve.

Cudjoe's Day

In order to help develop their new possessions, the Spanish, in the early 16th century, brought Africans as slaves to Jamaica, many were badly treated and so when the British invaded the island in 1655 most of them, determined not to be recaptured, sided against the newcomers and established themselves as Maroons living in gangs in the hills. They were, over the years, joined by further escaped slaves including one, Cudjoe, who soon became an outstanding leader in the Maroons' fight for freedom and independence. After many years of war the British offered to make peace, and the treaty of 1739 gave the Maroons land and limited self-rule.

The celebrations on January 6th commemorate Cudjoe's birthday and his signing of the Peace Treaty with the British. In the Cockpit Country in west Jamaica there is much feasting, singing and dancing, all accompanied by the beat of the Gumbay drum. A procession led by the Maroon Colonel winds its way to the Peace Cave where the treaty was signed, and then slowly returns, with many pauses to sing and dance and drum, to the village where the marchers disperse, leaving the drum on the parade ground for the night.

Gungo Pea Soup

Gungo or pigeon peas grow on a bush that can reach a height of 3 metres/10 feet. The peas, which are quite small, come in various colours from cream and green to deep purple, and there is a superstition that after shelling them it is lucky to keep an empty pod in your wallet. Canned peas can be used.

450g/1lb gungo peas
ham bone, saved from the Christmas ham
120g/4oz salt beef
4 spring onions, chopped
2 sprigs thyme
1 whole green scotch bonnet pepper
450g/1lb yam or cho-cho (choyote),
    peeled and diced
salt and pepper

1 Place the peas, ham bone and salt beef in a large pan and cover with water. Simmer for 1–1¼ hours, or until the peas are very soft, then add the spring onions, thyme, pepper and yam.
2 Simmer for a further 20–30 minutes or until the peas and yam are cooked through, then remove the pepper, thyme and ham bone, season to taste, and thin with a little more water, if necessary.

Bob Marley

The great Bob Marley, king of reggae music, Jamaica's modern hero whose influence has been so enormous, not only in the musical world but also through his dreams of equality of the races, has his own day : Bob Marley day (February 6th – his birthday) when a large celebration is held at the Bob Marley Museum in Hope Road, Kingston.

Marley, who died of cancer aged 36 in 1981, was a committed Rastafarian who brought little-known Jamaican 'roots' music to worldwide recognition. He sang of his belief in the inevitability of war unless equality of the races was recognised by all, and his records are still bought by fans everywhere.

It was in 1970 that Bob Marley and the Wailers established their own distinctive style and sound, and from then on nothing was to stop them in their transformation of reggae into a worldwide phenomenon that cut through the colour barrier and opened the way for succeeding generations. Marley continued his quest for peace and the historic concert in Jamaica in 1978 gave rise to the famous photograph of Mr Manley and Mr Seaga shaking hands while the peace maker, with dreadlocks flowing, belted out the 'One Love' theme. In the same year the United Nations awarded him the Medal of Peace.

Marley is now a legend and his thoughts, through his music, have influenced millions of teenagers worldwide, his double album made by his friend and promoter Chris Blackwell for the Island Records

label being the biggest selling of all time, with 10 million copies sold. The 'I-tal food' of the Rastafarians is the natural cooking of products from the earth without adding salt or preservatives. The letter 'I' appears in many Rasta words and signifies a divine sense of self with divine becoming I-vine and I-tal being a corruption of vital.

Rasta food, except for the occasional consumption of small fish, is entirely vegetarian, and the rich variety of local produce is used in stir-fries and vegetable stews, which are often thickened and flavoured with coconut milk, lime juice and hot pepper.

Vegetable Stir-Fry

2 tablespoons vegetable oil
2 cloves garlic, chopped
piece of ginger root, peeled and chopped
a selection of the following vegetables, chopped,
    sliced or grated: cauliflower, carrots, green beans,
    red pepper, celery, spring onions
1 teaspoon soy sauce
225ml/8fl oz/1 cup coconut milk
juice of half a lime
1 teaspoon hot pepper sauce

1 Heat the oil in a wok. Add the garlic and ginger and fry for 1 minute.
2 Add the vegetables one at a time, starting with the hard ones and finishing with the leafy ones. Stir continuously.
3 When the vegetables start to soften sprinkle on the soy sauce and stir in the coconut milk. Continue cooking for a few minutes, then add a squeeze of lime juice and the hot pepper sauce and serve immediately.

Stuffed Cho-Cho

If you can't get cho-cho or chayote use squash or courgette.

2 cho-chos (chayote)
1 tablespoon vegetable oil
2 spring onions, chopped
pinch of chopped scotch bonnet pepper,
  cored and deseeded
½ red pepper, cored, deseeded and chopped
4 tablespoons breadcrumbs
2 tablespoons coconut milk
juice of half a lime

1 Cut the cho-chos in half and remove the seeds.
Cook in boiling water for about 15 minutes, or until
tender. Carefully scoop out the flesh, reserving the
shells, chop finely.
2 Heat the oil in a frying pan and sauté the onions
and peppers. When soft remove from the heat and
mix in the cho-cho flesh and the remaining
ingredients.
3 Spoon the mixture into the cho-cho shells.
4 Bake at 180°C/350°F/gas 4 for
20 minutes, or until
light brown on top.

Matrimony

A favourite Jamaican dessert which is eaten in the spring when the star apple, a delightful Jamaican native fruit, is at its best.

4 star apples, seeded and sliced
2 oranges, peeled and sliced
¼ teaspoon grated nutmeg
6 tablespoons condensed milk

1 Mix the sliced fruit together, sprinkle with the nutmeg and then stir in the condensed milk.
2 Chill for 30 minutes before serving.

The Plantations

During the 18th century wealthy British sugar plantation owners began to build houses on their estates that were worthy of their life-style. They started by importing architects and engineers from Britain and Europe, and copied grand classical English Georgian and Italian Palladian architecture. The designs were altered slightly to accommodate the local conditions, and a style known as 'Jamaican Georgian' evolved. These wonderfully attractive and airy houses were constructed with the most important rooms on the first floor. Many were later deserted and then left to fall down. Some that were not destroyed by Hurricane Gilbert are being restored now.

Up at 7000ft in the beautiful Blue Mountains, a resort hotel called Strawberry Hill, owned by Bob Marley's promoter, Chris Blackwell, has recently been reconstructed. It consists of small villas resembling a traditional 19th-century Jamaican home (see end papers). These villas are magnificently sited with ravishing views over the surrounding countryside. Excellent food and comfort make a trip to Strawberry Hill a real treat.

Afficinados will tell you that Blue Mountain coffee with its subtle and aromatic flavour is the best in the world. Coffee was brought to Jamaica by the Governor, Sir Nicholas Lawes, in 1728 and seventy years later there were over 600 plantations. Today there are careful restrictions on who can call coffee Blue Mountain. It is a very important export for the island and now much of the best Blue Mountain coffee goes to the arbiters of good taste, the Japanese market. The locals not only savour and drink it, but often use it to flavour their desserts.

Tia Maria

Tia Maria of course is now world famous. It is a coffee based liqueur which was developed commercially after World War II as a drink for women when accompanying their beer-drinking husbands. It was made from the best Blue Mountain coffee by Englishmen led by Morris Cargill and named after one of his colleague's aunts, Mary. The impressive factory still manufactures the liqueur on the outskirts of Kingston.

Blue Mountain Coffee Chiffon

1½ tablespoons gelatine powder
3 tablespoons very strong hot coffee
2 tablespoons Tia Maria
4 eggs, separated
120g/4oz/½ cup caster sugar
300ml/10fl oz/1¼ cups light whipping cream
3 tablespoons freshly grated coconut, toasted

1 Sprinkle the gelatine over the hot coffee, leave
for 1 minute, then stir until dissolved.
2 In separate bowls whisk the egg whites and
the cream.
3 Whisk the egg yolks and the sugar together then
stir in the coffee.
4 Immediately, as the coffee mixture will set very
quickly, fold in first the cream and then the egg
whites. Turn into a bowl and chill well.
5 Sprinkle on the toasted coconut just before
serving.

Chinese New Year

Chinese colonies throughout the world have colourful and noisy celebrations for the Chinese New Year, and Jamaica is no exception. The date of the feast, in February or March, is calculated according to the lunar calendar, and the festival is now usually held on the nearest Sunday.

In Jamaica tradition has it that good fortune is brought by bathing in water containing the tea made from the leaves of a locally grown citrus fruit, the shaddock (pomelo). This ritual is followed by the cleansing of the palate when the fruit is squeezed and the juice drunk as a preliminary to the big feast. It is then time to eat and make merry. A large variety of both meat and vegetable dishes are served before the meal finishes with sweetmeats and cookies. All the while there is much music and entertainment, with colourful and decorative lanterns strung from the trees and dragon dances snaking and writhing down the streets.

Candied Shaddock Peel

The shaddock or pomelo is native to Southeast Asia and was probably brought to the Caribbean by the early Chinese immigrants.

1 shaddock
salt
450g/1lb/2 cups sugar, plus extra for rolling
2–3 slices ginger root

1 Peel the fruit, scrape away any pith on the inside of the peel, then cut the peel into matchsticks.
2 Place the peel in a pan of cold salted water and bring to the boil. Boil for 1 minute then drain and rinse under cold water. Repeat this boiling and rinsing process three times.
3 Place the sugar and ginger in a pan with 250ml/8fl oz/1 cup water over a gentle heat. When the sugar has all melted raise the heat and bring to the boil.
4 Add the peel and simmer gently for 30–40 minutes, or until the pieces of peel are translucent.
5 Remove from the heat, leave until cool, then transfer the peel to a rack to dry.
6 When completely dry roll the peel in sugar and store in an air-tight container.

Duckling in a Sweet-Sour Sauce

1 duck, cut into small serving pieces
6 heaped tablespoons cornflour
salt and pepper
1 egg, beaten
vegetable oil, for deep-frying
boiled rice, to serve

Doctorbird

Sauce
1 tablespoon cornflour
1 small can pineapple chunks, drained, juice reserved
soy sauce
2 tablespoons vinegar
45g/1½oz sugar
1 tablespoon molasses or black treacle
2 tablespoons vegetable oil
2 spring onions, chopped
1 green pepper, cored, deseeded and chopped
2 cloves garlic
crushed piece of ginger root, finely chopped
salt and pepper

1 To make the sauce, slake the cornflour in a little water, then blend with the juice from the pineapple, a good shake of soy sauce and the vinegar, sugar and molasses.
2 Heat the oil in a frying pan and gently fry the spring onions, pepper and garlic until soft. Add the cornflour mixture together with the ginger and pineapple pieces and 150ml/5floz/⅔ cup of water. Season well and simmer for 5 minutes.
3 Meanwhile, season the cornflour with salt and pepper. Dip the duck pieces into the egg and then coat with the seasoned cornflour.
4 Heat the oil in a deep-fryer and fry the duck pieces until brown and crisp. Drain well on kitchen paper.
5 Add the duck pieces to the sweet-sour sauce and simmer until tender. Serve on a bed of hot, fluffy rice.

Pagwa or Holi

An Indian festival that takes place, according to the lunar calendar, at full moon at the beginning of spring. It is really a Hindu festival, but in Jamaica Muslim Indians, as well as those of African descent, participate fully.

The story is that a miracle occurred after the battle in which the demon king gained victory over the gods. The king, whose son and daughter continued to worship the gods instead of him, ordered that they be burnt on a pyre. His son was burnt to ashes but his daughter was untouched, and the Holi fires are lit in remembrance of this. People gather round the log fires beating drums, singing chowtals (pagwa songs) and feasting on vegetarian dishes and sweet and spicy pastries.

This festival is colourful, and at times messy. Celebrants smear their faces and each other with brightly coloured powder and, as the festival continues, it is replaced by coloured water which is used to drench anybody within reach.

Aphelandra

25

Plantain Tarts

2 large, very ripe plantains
100g/3½oz/½ cup soft light brown sugar
½ teaspoon each nutmeg and mixed spice
1 teaspoon vanilla essence
225g/8oz shortcrust pastry

1 Preheat the oven to 200°C/400°F/gas 6.
2 Cook the plantains in boiling water for 10
minutes, then drain and peel. Mash the fruit and mix
in the sugar, spices and vanilla.
3 Roll out the pastry and cut into rounds of about
10cm/4in in diameter.
4 Put a heaped teaspoon of the mixture on each
pastry circle. Moisten the edge of the pastry with
cold water, then fold over to make half moons and
seal. Prick the tops with a fork. Bake the tarts for
20–25 minutes until golden brown.

Metai

These are crisp sweet pastries of the type much
loved by Indians everywhere.

225g/8oz/2 cups plain flour
½ teaspoon bicarbonate of soda
½ teaspoon salt
vegetable oil, for deep-frying

Syrup
450g/1lb/2 cups granulated sugar
300ml/½ pint/1¼ cups water

1 Sift together the flour, bicarbonate of soda and
salt and gradually add enough water to make a
stiff dough.
2 Knead well, then roll out the dough and cut into
finger-sized strips.

3 Heat the oil in a deep-fryer, add the dough strips in batches and fry until golden. Remove with a slotted spoon, drain on kitchen paper and keep warm.

4 Meanwhile, to make the syrup, place the sugar and water in a pan and boil until it forms a thick syrup.

5 Dip the cooked metai in the syrup then drain on a wire rack.

27

Easter

Christianity plays an important part in the life of many Jamaicans but Easter, especially for the older islanders, has a particular significance. Easter, with its symbolism of life emerging from death is, on the island, also associated with the emergence of freedom from slavery and it is at this time that families will meet and sit down and eat together.

Roast Suckling Pig

A suckling pig with its tender flesh makes a lovely party dish and will feed up to a dozen people. Occasionally, you may find a fresh one for sale, but it is more usual to buy them frozen. Make sure it is completely defrosted before cooking.

5kg/10lb suckling pig
vinegar
Stuffing
225g/8oz/1 cup rice
45g/1½oz butter
3 stalks celery, chopped
1 onion, peeled and chopped
¼ teaspoon chopped thyme leaves
apple juice
salt and pepper

1 To make the stuffing, boil the rice until tender, then drain well.

2 Heat the butter in a pan and sauté the celery, onion, garlic and thyme until soft. Stir in the rice, season to taste and add a little apple juice to moisten.

3 Stuff the pig with the rice mixture and close the cavity with metal skewers. Place a piece of wood in the pig's mouth and cover the ears and tail with foil to prevent them burning.

4 Roast the pig at 180°C/350°F/gas 4 for 1 hour, then lower the heat to 160°C/325°F/gas 3 and cook for another 3 hours, basting frequently.

5 To serve, remove the piece of wood and replace with an orange or apple.

Pepper Rum

A fiery hot rum which is used to spice up soups, stews or any dish that is considered bland. A few drops dribbled over the suckling pig would jazz it up no end, but be careful, as the rum is very hot.

1 bottle dark rum
1–2 scotch bonnet peppers
12 allspice Jamaican
    (pimento) berries
2 cloves
2 sprigs thyme

1 Pour about one-third of the bottle of rum into a jug.

2 Core and deseed the peppers, then cut into strips.

3 Put the peppers, allspice, cloves and thyme into the bottle and fill to the top with the reserved rum.

4 Seal tightly and keep the pepper rum in a dark place for at least 2 weeks before using.

Easter Spiced Bun

Many different varieties of bun are eaten around Easter time. This spiced one is very traditional and is usually served with cheese.

250ml/8fl oz/1 cup milk
225g/8oz/1½ cups demerara sugar
350g/12oz/3 cups plain flour
3 teaspoons baking powder
½ teaspoon salt
½ teaspoon grated nutmeg
2 teaspoons ground allspice (pimento)
150g/5½oz/1 cup raisins
2 eggs
15g/½oz butter or margarine, melted
1 teaspoon vanilla essence

1 Preheat the oven to 180°C/350°F/gas 4.
2 Heat the milk, add the sugar and stir until dissolved, then leave to cool.
3 Sift the dry ingredients together in a bowl and sprinkle in the raisins.
4 Beat the eggs, then whisk into the cooled milk with the melted butter and vanilla essence. Add to the dry ingredients and stir until mixed well.
5 Turn the mixture into a greased 750g/1½lb loaf tin and put into the hot oven. After 20 minutes reduce the temperature to 160°C/325°F/gas 3 and continue baking for another 45 minutes to an hour, or until a skewer inserted into the centre comes out clean.

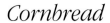

Cornbread

A great Jamaican favourite, this probably has as many recipes as there are cooks.

225g/8oz/1½ cups cornmeal
175g/6oz/1½ cups plain flour
½ teaspoon salt
3 teaspoons baking powder
2 eggs
120g/4oz/½ cup granulated sugar
250ml/8fl oz/1 cup vegetable oil
250ml/8fl oz/1 cup milk

1 Preheat the oven to 180°C/350°F/gas 4.
2 Combine the cornmeal, flour, salt and baking powder in a bowl.
3 In another bowl beat the eggs and sugar together, then stir in the oil and finally the milk. Stirring continuously, slowly pour the liquid into the flour mixture.
3 Pour the mixture into a greased 750g/1½lb loaf tin and bake for 50 minutes, or until cooked through.

Digging Match

In the rural communities, when a farmer needs help he calls on his friends and neighbours. On the chosen day all the villagers rally to his assistance. While the men get down to work, the women light fires and prepare the large meal that will be served later in the day.

Although the work may be backbreaking, the day is fun, and a singer-man or bomma, leads everybody in the robust singing of digging or work songs which combine well-known tunes with topical references. The workers' spirits are also kept up by drinking white rum, dispensed at intervals by a 'quarter-master'.

The meal will consist of one large and satisfying pot, served with dumplings or spinners and such dishes as roast breadfruit and ground yam, all washed down with a drink made out of sugar and water. Finally, everybody goes home happy and looking forward to the next time.

Jamaican Pepperpot Soup

The origins of this famous soup, with its local ingredients, go back to the Indians who inhabited the island before Columbus came. The Jamaican callaloo (Amaranthus) is different from the Trinidad callaloo (dasheen). Common names include Bush greens, Badi chauli and Kulitis. It can be bought in cans. If unavailable, use spinach instead.

750g/1½lb stewing steak
350g/12oz belly of pork, chopped
225g/8oz callaloo, roughly chopped
1kg/2lb kale, chopped
12 okra, cut into small rings
1 medium onion, chopped
3 spring onions, chopped
1 whole green scotch bonnet pepper
2 cloves garlic, crushed
2 sprigs thyme
125ml/4fl oz/½ cup
  coconut milk
salt and
  freshly
  ground
  black pepper

1 Place the stewing steak and belly of pork in a large pan of water. Bring to the boil and simmer for 30 minutes, or until the meat is almost tender.
2 Place the callaloo, kale and okra in another pan with a very little water. Cover and steam for 10 minutes, then add to the soup.
3 Add the onion, spring onions, pepper, garlic and thyme and, if the soup seems too thick, add more boiling water. Simmer for another hour, then remove the pepper.
4 Add the coconut milk, season to taste, stir well and cook for another 5 minutes.

Hussein/Hosay

This festival celebrates the triumph of good over evil
as represented in the fight between two brothers,
Hussein and Hosay. Like other Jamaican Indian
festivals, Hindus, Muslims and Jamaicans of all ethnic
origins participate. Central to a big procession is the
tazia, which is a minaret trimmed with coloured
paper decorations, stuck with hundreds of tiny and
shimmering mirrors, and topped with perhaps a
multi-coloured paper peacock with a long flowing
tail. This minaret is carried to a large open site
where singers, dancers, drummers and puppeteers
all perform. The climax comes as sunset approaches.
The puppets and *tazia* are carried in procession to
the river or sea and submerged in water, an act
which symbolises the ending of hostility and enmity.

Curry Goat

This dish is now more usually made with shoulder of lamb or mutton.

450g/1lb shoulder of lamb, cut into cubes
1 teaspoon curry powder, or to taste
¼ scotch bonnet pepper, deseeded and finely
  chopped
2 tablespoons vegetable oil
1 large potato, peeled and diced
salt and pepper
boiled rice, to serve

1 Place the meat in a bowl with the curry powder, onion, pepper and seasonings and mix well. Leave to marinade and cook for 20 minutes over a gentle heat, stirring frequently.
2 Add 250ml/8fl oz/1 cup water and the potatoes. Cover and cook over a low heat until the meat is tender and the gravy has thickened. Adjust the seasoning and serve very hot on a bed of boiled rice.
3 Accompany the curry with roti and at least two of the following: chutney, pickled beets, shredded coconut, raisins, chopped nuts and sliced bananas.

Roti or Chapati

120g/4oz/1 cup mixed wholewheat and plain flour
pinch of salt
3 tablespoons vegetable oil

1 Mix together the flours, salt and oil. Gradually add 175ml/6fl oz/¾ cup water, knead into a firm dough.
2 Divide the dough into 6 pieces. Roll into balls. Flatten the balls and roll into circles, 12cm/5in across.
3 Cook the roti on a heated griddle. Press them down and turn once or twice. They are cooked when brown and puffed up.

Emancipation

1ST AUGUST

Slavery finally came to an end on
1st August 1838, and that date
remained a holiday until the
Independence of Jamaica in 1962.
It was then decided to combine
the two with a national holiday
or Festival, which is held on the
first Monday in August. The day
is celebrated with a vast
spectrum of events including
fishing regattas, coconut
husking contests and the Miss
Jamaica pageant. A large
parade is also held, and that,
along with many bands, features
historical and mythical Jamaican
characters.

Stamp and Go

The unusual name for this dish of salted codfish
fritters is supposed to have derived from the 18th-
century British navy sailing ships. If an officer
wanted something to be done in a hurry the order
was 'Stamp and Go'.

450g/1lb saltfish
2 spring onions, chopped
½ teaspoon chopped scotch bonnet pepper, cored
   deseeded
½ teaspoon chopped thyme leaves
120g/4oz/1 cup plain flour
1 teaspoon baking powder
vegetable oil, for deep-frying

1 Soak the saltfish for several hours, then rinse and drain well. Place the fish in a pan of cold water and simmer for 15–20 minutes, then drain and remove all skin and bones.

2 Place the fish, spring onions, pepper and thyme in a food processor or blender and purée.

3 Add the flour, baking powder and enough water to make a thin batter.

4 Heat the oil in a deep-fryer and drop the mixture into it, one tablespoonful at a time. When the fritters are golden, remove with a slotted spoon and drain on kitchen paper.

Gizzadas

These coconut-filled tartlets with their crimped edges are also known as pinch-me-rounds and will feature in most picnic baskets on Emancipation Day.

225g/8oz shortcrust pastry
flesh from half a small coconut grated
90g/3oz/½ cup demerara sugar
½ teaspoon cinnamon
½ teaspoon ground ginger
½ teaspoon grated nutmeg

1 Mix all the ingredients bar the pastry together in a small pan, then stir in 3 tablespoons of water. Cook over a low heat stirring constantly, for about 5 minutes. Leave to cool.

2 Preheat the oven to 200°C/400°F/gas 6.

3 Roll out the pastry, cut into circles and use to line tart or muffin tins, crimping the edges with thumb and forefinger so that they stand up above the tin.

4 Spoon some of the coconut mixture into each one and bake for about 20 minutes, or until the pastry is golden and the coconut is starting to colour.

Jamaican Gingerbread

Jamaica is one of the world's largest producers of ginger, so it is not surprising that ginger features prominently in the local cuisine, with sticky gingerbread being a great favourite. The gingerbread is often decorated with a simple glaze of lime juice mixed with icing sugar.

225g/8oz/⅔ molasses or black treacle
120g/4oz/¾ cup of demerara sugar
120g/4oz/½ cup butter
3 tablespoons milk
½ teaspoon bicarbonate of soda
2 eggs
225g/8oz/2 cups plain flour
2 teaspoons chopped ginger root
5 knobs stem ginger, chopped
90g/3oz/½ cup raisins soaked in 2 tablespoons rum
   or orange juice
½ teaspoon each nutmeg and allspice

1 Preheat the oven to 160°C/325°F/gas 3 and grease a 20cm/8in cake tin.
2 Combine the molasses, sugar, butter and milk in a saucepan and heat gently to just melt the butter. Remove from the heat and stir in the bicarbonate of soda.
3 Allow to cool, then whisk in the eggs.
4 Add the remaining ingredients and stir, mix well.
5 Pour the batter into the tin and bake for 45–50 minutes, or until a skewer inserted in the middle comes out clean or, if you like it really sticky, nearly clean. Turn out on to a rack to cool, and decorate if desired.

Cricket

Drive round the towns or villages on any fine afternoon and every spare piece of grass or dirt yard will have been taken over by small boys to play cricket. Everyone is passionate about the game and families enjoy nothing more than a summer day's outing to watch a cricket match. A picnic or packed lunch might be the order of the day, otherwise there are many stalls selling fruit punch and freshly prepared meat patties, jerk pork and chicken.

Fruit Punch

This is made with freshly squeezed juice. The exact proportions are not absolutely crucial, but it does need the lemon or lime.

250ml/8fl oz/1 cup grapefruit juice
500ml/16fl oz/2 cups orange juice
50ml/2fl oz/¼ cup lemon or lime juice
175g/6oz/¾ cup granulated sugar, or to taste

Mix together, adding more sugar if liked, and topping up with iced water to taste.

Jerk Chicken

Lady Nugent, whose husband was British Governor of Jamaica, wrote a journal about her time on the island between 1801 and 1805. It is a fascinating account of her life, travels and thoughts, usually very moral, about Jamaica and its people. She gives a description of a banquet she attended up in the Moro which had 'jerked hog' as the centrepiece, saying it was a way of dressing the meat of the Maroons. The name of Lady Nugent lives on in the commercially produced foods bearing her name, marketed by Grace Foods Ltd.

In fact, Jerk originally came from the Indians and was developed by the Maroons as a way of preserving the meat of wild hog both for their own consumption and to sell to passing ships.

The meat is smothered in jerk paste and then left to marinate for several hours. Nowadays it is cooked on a barbecue, but originally a pit was dug with a grill made of young green sticks balanced on stones over the top and the meat was cooked very slowly, or virtually smoked, over the dying embers of a fire made of pimento (allspice) wood.

1.5kg/3lb chicken, jointed
½ scotch bonnet pepper, cored, deseeded and chopped
1 tablespoon fresh thyme leaves
1 tablespoon finely chopped ginger root
½ teaspoon each nutmeg and cinnamon
2 cloves garlic, crushed
3 spring onions, chopped
2 teaspoons ground allspice (pimento)
2 teaspoons lime juice or vinegar
2 tablespoons vegetable oil
salt and pepper

1 Place all the ingredients except the chicken in a blender or food processor and purée.
2 Prick the chicken pieces all over with a sharp knife, then rub them generously with the jerk paste. Leave to marinate overnight or for 24 hours.
3 Light your barbecue and let the flames die down before cooking. Turn the chicken once or twice and when brown all over put on a cool area of the grill and leave for at least 30 minutes, or until the juices run clear when tested with a skewer.

Harvest Festival

Harvest Festival is widely observed as a thanksgiving to God for the safe gathering and reaping of the year's crops. It takes place in September or October, and dishes made of the mellow autumn fruits and vegetables such as pumpkins and sweet potatoes predominate at the meal, which is eaten after the church service.

Sweet Potato Pone

This sweet potato pudding, or pone as it is called locally, can be eaten hot, when the centre will be gooey and runny, or left until cold and cut as a cake.

750g/1½lb sweet potatoes
120g/4oz/1 cup plain flour
750ml/1¼ pint/3 cups coconut milk
225g/8oz/1⅓ cups demerara sugar
2 teaspoons vanilla essence
1½ teaspoons ground cinnamon
1 teaspoon grated nutmeg
1 teaspoon ground ginger
225g/8oz/1½ cups raisins
20g/¾oz butter, melted

Topping
2 tablespoons each of coconut oil and honey

1 Preheat the oven to 180°C/350°F/gas 4.
2 Peel and grate the sweet potato. Mix with the flour, then stir in all the other ingredients.
3 Pour the mixture into a well greased 20cm/8in square baking tin. Mix together the coconut oil and honey and drizzle over the top.
4 Bake in the preheated oven for 1¼ hours, or until well browned and cooked.

Soursop Ice-Cream

Soursop is a native Jamaican fruit that was originally cultivated by the Taino Indians for its medicinal properties. It has an interesting and distinctive taste and is much used in cooling drinks or, as here, in ice-cream.

1 ripe soursop
pinch of salt
1 small can evaporated milk
1 small can condensed milk

1 Peel the soursop.
Place the flesh in a
blender with
600ml/1 pint/
2½ cups water
and purée.
2 Strain, extracting as
much juice as possible.
3 Stir the milks and the
juice together, pour into a container and freeze in the usual way.

Mango Cheese

The mango tree came to Jamaica from the East Indies towards the end of the 18th century. The ship arrived with many trees of several different varieties, which were numbered rather than named, when planted. These numbers are still used, with number 11 and number 32 being the most popular. Mango cheese is a very popular candy which is eaten on its own, or with a fresh, salty dairy cheese.

3 ripe mangoes
lime juice
450–740g/1–1½lb/2–3 cups granulated sugar

1 Peel and stone the mangoes, then purée the flesh in a blender or food processor.
2 Measure the purée, and for each 225g/8oz/1 cup add ½ teaspoon lime juice and ¾ cup sugar.
3 Place in a heavy pan and bring to the boil. Boil rapidly, stirring constantly, for 25–30 minutes, or until the mixture comes away easily from the sides of the pan.
4 Pour the mixture into a greased 20cm/8in square tin. Leave to set, then cut into squares.

Roasted Garden Egg Purée

In Jamaica aubergines have the charming name of garden eggs. This delicious purée can be used as a stuffing for tomatoes or squash or eaten as a dip, when it is often served with freshly made plantain chips. Deep fried in oil.

2 garden eggs, peeled and sliced lengthwise
½ teaspoon finely chopped scotch bonnet pepper, cored and deseeded
4 cloves garlic, crushed
2 spring onions, chopped
1 tablespoon fresh thyme leaves
3 tablespoons vinegar
4 tablespoons vegetable oil
2 teaspoons soy sauce
salt and pepper

1 Place the garden egg slices in a shallow dish. Mix all the remaining ingredients together and spread over the slices. Leave to marinate for 2–3 hours.
2 Cook in a medium 180°C/350°F/gas 4 oven for 30 minutes, or until the slices are tender and cooked through.
3 Purée the slices in a blender or food processor, turn into a bowl and season to taste.

Nine Night

On the ninth day after a death family and friends gather at the house of the deceased to cheer the bereaved. Songs are sung, often serious, but always full of hope, and designed to help the departing spirit across the 'river'. These are usually accompanied by a small percussion band and a boom pipe (a length of bamboo which is blown).

Very traditional foods are served with coffee and rum punch and, and as the evening wears on, mugs of hot, spicy chocolate are drunk.

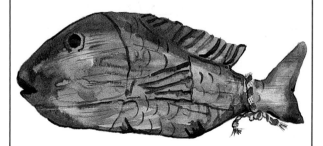

Escovitch Fish

This dish of fried fish marinated in hot escovitch sauce is eaten either warm or cold, and is traditionally accompanied by bammies (see page 47).

450g/1lb white fish fillets
flour, for coating
2 tablespoons vegetable oil
2 bay leaves
½ scotch bonnet pepper, cored and deseeded

125ml/4fl oz/½ cup malt vinegar
1 onion, sliced
4 allspice (pimento) berries
2.5cm/1in piece ginger root, peeled and sliced
salt and pepper

1 Cut the fish into strips and sprinkle with flour.
2 Heat the oil in a frying pan, fry the fish until
golden brown; remove from the pan and cool.
3 Place all the remaining ingredients in a pan, add
225ml/8fl oz/1 cup water and bring to the boil.
4 Simmer until the onion is cooked, then pour the
hot sauce over the cooked fish. Leave to soak for an
hour or two, and serve.

Bammies

Bammies are make from the cassava root. This is
another of the Jamaican dishes that are known to
have been eaten by the Arawak Indians.

1kg/2lb bitter cassava
pinch of salt
coconut milk, for soaking
butter, for spreading

1 Peel and grate the cassava. Place in a muslin cloth
and wring out all the juice. Mix with a pinch of salt.
2 Place about a quarter of the mixture in a small
greased frying pan and press down to flatten.
3 Cook over a moderate heat and when the edges
start to shrink, turn the bammy over to cook the
other side. Repeat with the remaining mixture.
4 Place the bammies in a shallow bowl filled with
coconut milk and leave to soak for 10 minutes.
5 Remove the bammies from the bowl and drain on
kitchen paper. Grill the bammies until light brown,
then spread them with butter and serve with the
escoveitch fish.

Nanny Day

Nanny is Jamaica's only woman national hero, having been one of the most feared Maroon warriors in the guerilla wars against the British. She was a brilliant military strategist and leader whose prowess gained her the reputation of having superhuman powers in a battle.

She is revered by the Eastern Maroons of Portland, who call her 'Grandy Nanny' and her day, the date of which is designated by the Maroon Colonel, is celebrated with feasting, drumming, singing and dancing.

The eating of the kernels of cacoon nuts is especially significant since it was the branches of these trees that were used to camouflage Maroon warriors in the wars against the British. They used the Spanish word 'aqui', now ackee, for the national fruit of Jamaica, according to Lady Nugent's diary.

Mussel (or Buzzu) Soup

A buzzu is a river mussel which the Moore Town Maroons pick from the Rio Grande and Priestmans rivers, preferably on a Saturday night when there is a full moon.

3.5–4.8 litres/3–4 quarts fresh mussels
a selection of the following: pieces of yam, green
  bananas, breadfruit, coco and spinners (page 61)
2–3 spring onions
sprig thyme
1 whole scotch bonnet pepper
salt and pepper

1 Scald the mussels in boiling water, drain and remove the meat from the shells.
2 Bring a large pan of water to the boil, then add

the selection of fruit, vegetables and spinners. Add
the shelled mussels.
3 When everything is nearly cooked add the spring
onions, thyme, scotch bonnet pepper and salt and
pepper.
4 Simmer for a few minutes, then remove the
seasonings and serve very hot.

Dukunu

This dish of banana skins wrapped round a starch
filling originally came from West Africa. It has the
nice local name of 'blue drawers' because the
wrapping of banana leaves gives a bluish stain to the
filling. It is also known as 'tie a leaf', which refers to
the parcels being tied up with strips of banana bark.
Foil can be used as a substitute for banana leaves.

150g/5oz/1 cup
   cornmeal
120g/4oz/1 cup
   plain flour
2 teaspoon nutmeg,
   grated
150g/5oz/1 cup
   demerara sugar
2 tablespoons raisins
120ml/8fl oz/1 cup coconut milk
banana leaves

1 Mix together the cornmeal, flour, nutmeg, sugar
and raisins. Stir in enough coconut milk to give a
dropping consistency.
2 Dip the banana leaves in boiling water to make
them pliable.
3 Spoon the mixture onto squares of banana leaves
and tie into parcels with banana bark or string. Place
in boiling water and simmer for 45 minutes.
4 Serve hot with rum butter or orange sauce.

Orange Sauce

1 tablespoon arrowroot or cornflour
juice of 2 oranges
60g/2oz granulated sugar
½ teasoon grated orange zest
1 tablespoon rum (optional)

1 Put the arrowroot or cornflour in a small bowl and gradually stir in the orange juice. Stir in the sugar and orange zest.
2 Transfer the mixture to a pan and bring slowly to the boil, stirring constantly.
3 When the sauce thickens remove from the heat and add the rum, if using.
4 Serve warm with the dukunu.

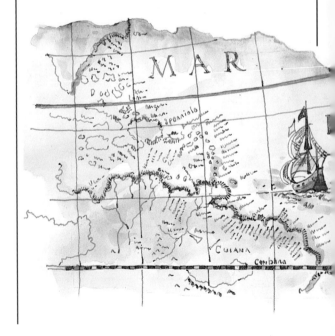

Hannukah

The original Jewish settlers in Jamaica were Portuguese and arrived with Christopher Columbus. After emancipation and the ending of slavery, the Jewish community was enlarged by the arrival of merchants from both Syria and the Lebanon. These groups are still well represented in business and, although their influence on the local food has not been significant, the Jews are credited with having introduced the aubergine – or garden egg as it is known in Jamaica – to the island.

The famous defeat of the Greeks by Judas Maccabaeus and his followers is celebrated during the eight days of Hannukah. There are many parties and large dinners and, especially for the children, presents. Hannukah, the feast of lights, usually falls in December and is on the 25th day of Kislev, the 9th month according to the lunar calendar.

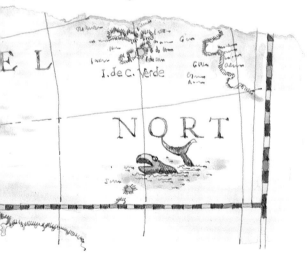

Potato Pancakes

Potato pancakes (latkes) were originally made with cream cheese, but as this was not available in northern climes in December the Jewish population in Russia, and now the Jamaicans, substitute potatoes for the cheese. This is how they are now made. For the festival they are served alongside the main course, but they are also frequently eaten on their own, accompanied by an apple sauce or sour cream.

4 large potatoes
2 eggs
2 tablespoons very finely chopped onion
2 tablespoons breadcrumbs
salt and pepper
vegetable oil, for frying

1 Peel the potatoes and grate finely so that they are almost a pulp. Put the potatoes into a sieve and squeeze out the liquid.
2 Beat the eggs, then add the grated potatoes and other ingredients and mix together.
3 Pour oil into a frying pan to a depth of 1cm/½in. Heat the pan and when the oil is hot drop in tablespoonfuls of the mixture, flattening the cakes with the back of a spoon.
4 Cook for about 5 minutes, until the pancakes are a rich brown underneath, then turn and cook the other side until it is also brown. Drain on paper towels and serve immediately.

Doughnuts

225g/8oz/1 cup plain flour
2 teaspoons baking powder
¼ teaspoon each cinnamon, cloves and mace
½ teaspoon salt

90g/3oz/⅓ cup caster sugar, plus extra for sprinkling
70g/2½oz/¼ cup margarine
1 egg
60ml/2fl oz/¼ cup milk
vegetable oil, for deep-frying

1 Mix the flour, baking powder, spices and salt.
2 Cream the sugar and margarine until smooth then
mix in the egg and milk. Make a well in the centre of
the flour and pour in the sugar mixture. Mix
thoroughly together.
3 Turn out the dough onto a floured board and roll
out to 1cm/½in thick.
4 Heat the oil in a deep-fryer to 180°C/350°F. Cut
out the dough with a doughnut cutter and deep-fry,
a few at a time, until golden. Drain on kitchen paper
and sprinkle with sugar while hot.

Orange Grenadine

A simple fruit salad that makes a very refreshing
dessert at the end of a large Hannukah dinner.

for each person:
1 very large orange
granulated sugar
grenadine syrup
lemon juice

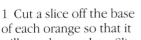

1 Cut a slice off the base
of each orange so that it
will stand on a plate. Slice off a lid about a third of
the way down from the top.
2 Using a grapefruit knife, loosen the sections of
fruit and remove the central core of pith.
3 Spoon in sugar to fill the centre of the orange,
then soak it with grenadine syrup.
4 Sprinkle a little lemon juice over the top. Replace
the lid and refrigerate until ready to serve.

Christmas

At Christmas the slaves and plantation workers were given, by law, at least three days holiday – this was often their only break in the entire year. As a result, there is still a feeling on the island that the festival has particular significance, though the street processions which were led by prancing masqueraders in amazing costumes have now all died out. These processions were accompanied in some areas by drum and fife, and in other places praise and derision songs were accompanied in a rhythmic style by three drums. These drums, the bass, the fundeh and the repeater, are the ones now often used by the Rastafarians, following Bob Marley's lead.

Feasting was always part of the Christmas celebrations and in old Jamaica smoked pork was the centrepiece to the meal. This pork was hung on a special metal hook, known as a kreng-kreng, over an open fire inside the house and then smoked gradually over several months, to be perfect at Christmas. However, Christianity gradually gained supremacy over the African-based festivities and the holiday is now traditionally spent with carol-singing, church services, giving presents and eating Christmas dinner at home with the family.

Rice and Peas

A favourite dish that also has the nickname 'Jamaican Coat of Arms', it is the centrepiece of many festive meals and is usually made with red kidney beans. At Christmas or New Year these are replaced with canned gungo peas or red kidney beans.

flesh of 1 coconut, grated, or 450ml/16fl oz/2 cups
   coconut milk
225g/8oz/1 cup gungo peas, soaked overnight
2 cloves garlic, chopped
350g/12oz/2 cups rice, rinsed
1 medium onion, peeled and chopped
3 spring onions
2 or 3 sprigs thyme
1 teaspoon hot scotch bonnet pepper sauce
salt

1 If using grated coconut combine it with 450ml/
16floz/2 cups hot water and squeeze the milk out
through a sieve. Add the same amount of water and
repeat the process. Discard the coconut but keep
the milk.
2 Drain and rinse the peas. Place them in a pan with
the garlic and coconut milk, bring to the boil and
simmer gently for about 1 hour, until tender.
3 Add the rice and the onion and season with salt.
Add enough water to cover the rice well, then place
the spring onions, thyme sprigs and scotch bonnet
pepper sauce on top of the rice.
4 Cover the pan, bring to the boil and simmer
gently for 20 minutes. Remove the spring onions,
thyme and pepper, stir with a fork and continue
cooking until the rice is fluffy.

Egg Nog

4 eggs
125ml/4fl oz/½ cup cream
120g/4oz/½ cup granulated sugar
250ml/8fl oz/1 cup light rum
450ml/16fl oz/2 cups milk
soda water, to taste
grated nutmeg, to sprinkle

1 Process the eggs, cream, sugar, rum and half the milk in a blender or food processor.
2 Pour into a jug, stir in the rest of the milk and put into the refrigerator to chill.
3 To serve, pour into glasses and top up with soda water to taste. Sprinkle grated nutmeg over the top.

Christmas Sorrel Drink

The red poinsettia is Jamaica's most widespread Christmas symbol. They grow everywhere and can be seen both in the wild and cultivated in gardens and in pots. Also, there are the crimson flowers of the sorrel bush, used to make this bright red drink.

3–4 large pieces of root ginger
1kg/2lb/8 cups sorrel sepals
6 cloves
8 allspice (pimento) berries
about 225g/8oz/1 cup granulated sugar
250ml/8fl oz/1 cup white rum

1 Peel the ginger and bruise it with a rolling pin.
2 Place the sorrel, ginger, cloves and allspice in a large bowl and cover with boiling water. Leave to stand overnight, then strain, sweeten to taste and stir in the rum.
3 Decant into bottles and refrigerate for a few days before drinking.

Rum Butter

Jamaican Christmas puddings have a wonderfully rich and subtle flavour because the dried fruit is soaked in rum for at least a month, and sometimes as long as a year, before being steamed in the pudding. They are served with rum butter.

225g/8oz/1 cup butter
225g/8oz/2 cups icing sugar
50ml/2fl oz/¼ cup dark rum
¼ teaspoon ground cinnamon

1 Cream the butter with a wooden spoon. Add the sugar, rum and cinnamon and mix well together.
2 Turn into a small bowl or dish and refrigerate until set.

Ettu Table

The Ettu people trace their ancestry to the Yorubas who came from Nigeria during the early days of slavery. The group is fast dwindling, but beliefs and practices are strongly in evidence in certain isolated areas in Western Jamaica.

Ettu Soup

Annatto seeds, which are virtually tasteless, give this soup a bright orange colour. They contain a powerful dye, the source of 'war paint' for the American Indians. Enslaved Africans used them in cooking to simulate the rich colour of palm oil. Use saffron or turmeric instead. Bady heart is the edible root of a member of the lily family but it can be replaced by the local callaloo or spinach. The soup is not seasoned with salt as salt is supposed to weaken the diner spiritually.

225g/8oz lamb or beef, chopped
225g/8oz chopped bady heart, callaloo or spinach
6 medium okra, sliced
½ teaspoon annatto seeds (or 2–3 strands saffron)
a few allspice Jamaican (pimento) berries
2–3 sprigs thyme

1 Simmer the meat in about 1 litre/1¾ pints of water, and when it starts to break up add the remaining ingredients.
2 Continue to simmer until everything is cooked. The okra will thicken the soup and give it good texture.

Foo-Foo

These are dipped into the soup before being eaten.

2 plantains
30g/1oz soft butter
1 tablespoon rum (optional)
salt and pepper

1 Boil the plantains for about 30 minutes, or until tender. Peel the fruit and purée.
2 Add the butter and rum and season to taste.
3 Mould into small balls, place them on a baking sheet and heat in a moderate oven for 5 minutes.

Natta Cho-Cho

Vibrant red annatto oil is made by adding a spoonful of annatto seeds to some hot oil, and straining them when the oil is cold. Use chilli oil if you cannot get annatto oil.

2 cho-cho (chayote), peeled and deseeded
4 tablespoons annatto oil
salt and pepper

1 Cut the cho-chos into julienne strips.
2 In heated oil, sauté the cho-cho for 3–5 minutes.
3 Drain, season, and serve immediately.

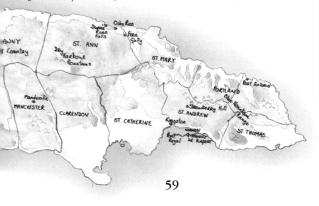

Kumina Duty

The Kumina people or 'Free Africans' came to Jamaica from the Congo and Angola in the post-abolition period last century. They were quickly assimilated into Jamaica's cultural potpourri, but even today they often communicate in their own Kikongo language, especially if strangers are present.

Rituals and ceremonies are known as Duties and the New Year Kumina Duty asks the supreme God to forgive past sins and to bestow blessings on the year to come. Preparations last for many days and include the baking of special loaves of bread, and the careful cleansing of the people and the goat which is to be sacrificed.

The ceremony revolves round the Kumina Queen who invokes spiritual help by fervently singing and dancing throughout the night. At midnight the goat is sacrificed, and the drumming and singing continue while the sacrificed animal is cooked down into the famous soup known as Mannish Water. Mannish Water has the reputation of enhancing a man's virility and is served to bridegrooms on their wedding night. Traditionally, it is cooked for a minimum of 50 people, in a 5-gallon drum balanced on top of stones with a fire underneath. It consists of the goat's meat, head and feet, slowly stewed with spices, vegetables, chopped up green bananas and dumplings, with a generous amount of overproof rum stirred in.

These dumplings, known as spinners, are simply made from a dough of flour, water and a little salt. The dough is rolled into small sausages which are dropped into the soup about 20 minutes before serving so they can cook through.

Johnny Cakes

Johnny cakes or journey cakes are universally popular, and freshly-made ones can be bought at roadside stands all over the island.

175g/6oz/1½ cups flour
1 teaspoon baking powder
¼ teaspoon salt
30g/1oz margarine
250ml/8fl oz/1 cup coconut oil

1 Sift together the flour, baking powder and salt, then rub in the margarine.
2 Bind with enough cold water to form a soft dough and knead well. Divide and shape into 10 balls.
3 Heat the oil in a pan, and fry the cakes in hot oil until brown on both sides.
4 Remove with a slotted spoon and drain on kitchen paper. Serve hot.

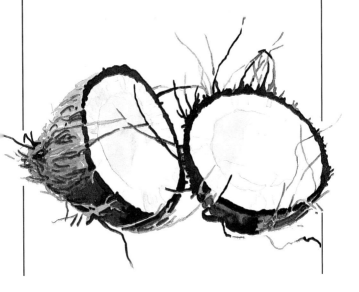

62